MAINE

in words and pictures

BY DENNIS B. FRADIN

ILLUSTRATIONS BY RICHARD WAHL

MAPS BY LEN W. MEENTS

Consultant:
Dean P. Bennett, Ph.D.
Project Director
Maine Studies Curriculum Project
Department of Educational & Cultural Services
Augusta, Maine

  CHILDRENS PRESS ™

CHICAGO

Cape Elizabeth

Library of Congress Cataloging in Publication Data

Fradin, Dennis B.
  Maine in words and pictures.

  SUMMARY: Presents a brief history and
description of the Pine Tree State.
  1.   Maine—Juvenile literature.   [1.   Maine]
I.   Wahl, Richard, 1939-   II.   Meents, Len W.
III.   Title.
F19.3.F69   974.1   79-25122
ISBN 0-516-03919-9

Picture Acknowledgments:
MAINE STATE DEVELOPMENT OFFICE—cover, pages 2, 5, 12, 20, 22,
26, 27, 28, 31, 33, 34, 35, 40
MAINE MARITIME MUSEUM, BATH, MAINE—11, 19, 37, 38, 42
ARCHITECT OF THE U.S. CAPITOL—page 8 ("Leiv Eriksson Discovers
America," by Per Krohg [1936] after Christian Krohg [1893]).
COVER—Pemaquid Lighthouse

Maine is nicknamed the *Pine Tree State*. Trees cover about 90 percent of the state. Long ago, Indians used Maine trees to make canoes. Later, the English cut down Maine trees to build ships. Today, wood and paper come from Maine forests. These forests are also home to many moose, bears, deer, and other animals.

The northeastern part of the United States is called *New England*. It includes the states of Connecticut, Maine, Massachusetts, New Hampshire, Rhode Island, and Vermont. Maine is the biggest state in New England. It lies on the Atlantic Ocean. There are lighthouses and harbors along the beautiful rocky coast. Because of the ocean, Maine is a leading fishing state. Maine is also a leading potato-growing state.

Maine has much more than forests, fishing, potatoes, and beautiful scenery.

Do you know where the sun's light first falls on the United States each morning?

Do you know where Vikings are thought to have explored in about the year 1000?

Do you know where most of the blueberries eaten in the United States are grown?

As you will learn, the answer to all these questions is the Pine Tree State—Maine.

Over a million years ago the Ice Age began. Huge mountains of ice, called *glaciers* (GLAY • shurz), covered Maine. Glaciers helped shape the land. They scooped out deep holes and scratches in the earth. Melting glaciers later filled these with water. Now they are lakes and rivers. Glaciers were so heavy that much of the coast sank into the ocean. Hilltops off the new coast poked out of the water. They had become islands.

Monhegan Island off the coast of Maine

We believe that there were people in Maine 10,000 years ago. Among the first people in Maine were the *Red Paint People*. They lived in Maine about 4,000 years ago. They made boats. They fished in Maine waters. It is thought that they hunted deer and gathered berries. They buried their dead with a red clay. That is why they are called the Red Paint People. This clay is thought to have come from Mount Katahdin (kah • TAH • din) in Maine. Little is known about these long-ago people, however.

When the early European explorers arrived in Maine they found many groups of Indians. The Indians belonged to two main groups. The Etchemin (ECH • ih • min) Indians lived east of the Penobscot (pen • AHB • scot) River. The Abnaki (ahb • NAH • kee) group of Indians made their villages west of the Penobscot River.

In the spring, the Indians of Maine fished for salmon. They planted corn and beans near the banks of Maine rivers. During the summer some went to the ocean to hunt for seals and porpoises. They ate the meat. They used the skins for making clothes.

In the fall, the Indians harvested their crops. They hunted for deer in the woods. Near Christmastime Maine Indians held a big thanksgiving feast. They enjoyed cranberries and turkey.

During the cold Maine winters the Indians wore snowshoes for travel. They hunted moose. They tapped maple trees for sap. The Indians in Maine were fine artists. They made baskets and pottery. They carved pipes. They also made fishnets and bows and arrows. All these can be seen today in Maine museums. But the coming of the white men largely destroyed the Indian way of life.

Painting of Viking explorer Leif Ericson discovering America

It is thought that Viking explorers (from the area of Norway) were the first outsiders in Maine. Leif Ericson (LEEF AIR • ick • son) was called "Leif the Lucky." We think he explored the Atlantic coast in about the year 1000. This may have been the first exploration on the mainland of North America. Later, other Viking explorers came. They may have hunted and fished along the Atlantic coast. These early Viking explorers were not interested in settling America. One reason they came to America was to get timber for building ships.

It was hundreds of years before explorers returned to the area. Over the years, explorers from England, Norway, Italy, Spain, and France explored the coast. In 1497 Italian explorer John Cabot was sent across the Atlantic Ocean by the king of England. Many people think he explored the Maine area between 1497 and 1499. In 1524 Giovanni da Verrazano (jo • VAH • nee dah vair • uh • TZAH • no), sailing for France, explored Maine. In 1569 three English sailors journeyed beyond the coast onto Maine soil. In 1605 English Captain George Weymouth (WAY • muth) arrived in Maine. He kidnapped five Indians. He brought them back to England. Many Maine Indians had helped the newcomers to survive in this new land. Now many grew to hate the white men.

Both England and France had explored the Maine area. Both England and France claimed the land. In 1604 Frenchman Samuel de Champlain (sham • PLANE) had explored the biggest island off the Maine coast. He called it *L'Isle des Monts Deserts* (LEEL day MOHN day • ZAIR) — Mount Desert. The French built several small settlements in Maine. French fur traders arrived. They gave pots, knives, and trinkets to the Indians. In return the Indians gave them valuable furs. French priests also came to Maine. They wanted to turn the Indians into Christians.

The English built settlements, too. Maine provided England with wood for ships. In 1607 the English formed the Popham Colony at the mouth of the Kennebec (KEN • eh • beck) River. These settlers returned to England the next spring, however. The winter had been bitter cold and their leader had died.

Model of the *Virginia,* a pinnace built by members of the Popham Colony.

In 1614 Captain John Smith explored Maine for England. In the 1620s the English built more settlements. By 1641 the English had built the city of Gorgeana (gore • jee • AN • ah). It is now called York. It was the first English city chartered by law in land that is now the United States.

"The land is ours!" said the English. They claimed a large area of America.

"It is ours!" said the French.

"We were here first," said the Indians.

For almost 100 years the French, the Indians, and the English fought fiercely. They were fighting over a large piece of land in America. This land included Maine. Some Indians helped the English. Others helped the French. In 1763 England won these wars. They were known as the French and Indian Wars. Now the English ruled in Maine.

More English settlers came to Maine. They cut down trees. They built wooden houses, churches, and schools. They built towns. Some of these towns were Kittery, Wells, and Berwick. Many people who lived near the ocean fished. Farther inland, settlers farmed. They

Fishing and lobster boats at Casco Bay

planted corn and beans. They tapped maple trees for sap. They hunted deer. They made deerskin clothes. Many towns held town meetings. At the meetings the people decided how to solve their problems.

In the 1760s many people in the English colonies were growing angry at England. The English king made them pay large taxes. The king ruled them. He made laws for them.

American people decided to free themselves from England. "Let's form a new country—the United States of America!" many said. In 1774 people from nine Maine towns met in Falmouth (FAL • mith) Falmouth is now Portland. They met to protest the taxes. Some Maine people burned the tax bills. Also in 1774 Maine settlers burned some English tea at York. This was called the *York Tea Party*. Much more than tea was involved. The people were showing the English that Americans wanted to be free.

Fighting between England and the American colonies started on April 19, 1775. This was the beginning of the Revolutionary War. At Valley Forge (FORJ), there were more than 1,000 Maine men in George Washington's army. There were sea battles on the waters along the Maine coast.

English ships fired on Maine's coastal cities. On October 18, 1775, Falmouth was pounded with cannonballs and bombs. Almost all the buildings were burned. Grele's Tavern survived the attack. It was owned by a woman named Alice Grele. When the tavern caught fire, Alice Grele filled her pots and pans with water. She took them to her roof. She put the fire out. Alice Grele came to represent the tough (TUFF) independence of Maine people.

Also in 1775 the *Margaretta* (mar • gahr • ET • ah), an English ship, was sailing off the coast of Maine near Machias (mah • CHY • us). The *Margaretta* had sixteen big guns. In a smaller ship, the *Unity*, Americans attacked the *Margaretta*. The *Unity* had no cannon or big guns. The *Unity* drew alongside the *Margaretta*. The English soldiers had bayonets. The American sailors were farmers and fishermen. They had pitchforks and a few guns. Yet the Americans won the fight. The *Margaretta* was captured. It was taken to Machias. This battle is often called the first naval battle of the Revolutionary War.

In 1783 the Americans won the Revolutionary War. The United States of America had been born.

Maine was not a state at first. It was part of the state of Massachusetts (mass • ah • CHOO • sets). More and more people came to Maine. Between 1764 and 1810 the population jumped from about 97,000 to about 229,000. Revolutionary War soldiers were given land in Maine. Some came to farm. They chopped down trees and built log cabins. Towns were built farther and farther inland.

By the early 1800s, lumbering was a big business. There were millions and millions of pine trees in Maine. Many were used for shipbuilding. Strong men called *lumberjacks* chopped down the trees. The trees were cut into logs. The logs were dragged by oxen to rivers. All winter the logs sat by the rivers. When the ice melted, the "spring drives" began. The lumber was floated down the rivers to the sawmills. Sometimes there were log jams. Then the strongest lumberjacks had to pull the logs apart with poles. The trees were like green gold. At one time, a single perfect tree could be sold for as much as a thousand dollars. A perfect tree could be made into a ship's mast. It seemed that there would always be plenty of trees.

By 1815 many Maine people wanted Maine to become a separate state. They did not want to be a part of Massachusetts. They hadn't liked being taxed by England. They didn't like being taxed by Massachusetts. They wanted more say in their government. In 1819 Maine people voted to become a separate state. On March 15, 1820, Maine became our twenty-third state. Portland was the first capital. Augusta was made capital in 1832. Maine was nicknamed the Pine Tree State. Pine trees were important to Maine.

Early fishermen had called the mainland of the state *The Main*. They thought of it as separate from the islands off the shore. We think that this is how Maine got its name.

Canada and Maine had argued about the border since 1783. Real fighting almost broke out. But the 1839 "Aroostook (ah • ROOS • tuck) War" over the border was fought mostly with words. The Webster-Ashburton Treaty of 1842 set the present boundary.

Island off the coast of Maine

Maine people had always valued freedom. They freed themselves from England. They freed themselves from Massachusetts. Most Maine people were against slavery. Hannibal Hamlin was against slavery. He was elected governor of Maine in 1857. In the South, black people were used as slaves.

Slavery was one of the big issues during the Civil War (1861-1865). During the Civil War, the Northern states fought the Southern states. About 73,000 Maine men fought on the side of the North. During the Civil War, Hannibal Hamlin was vice president of the United States. Abraham Lincoln was president.

The Civil War ended with the North beating the South. Slavery was ended.

After the Civil War, there was a terrible fire in Portland. The fire started on the Fourth of July, 1866. The city was almost destroyed. Portland was rebuilt. It has become Maine's biggest city.

Lumbering, farming, and fishing boomed after the Civil War. In the 1890s Maine's Aroostook County became an important potato-growing area. By the 1920s Aroostook County farmers were also raising milk cows and chickens.

Aroostook County potato harvest

In the 1890s dams were built in Maine. These dams keep the rivers from flooding. They also help turn waterpower into electricity.

During World War I (1914-1918) over 35,000 Maine men and women fought for the United States. During World War II (1939-1945) many ships were built in Maine shipyards. Combat ships were built. So were submarines. In 1956, one of the first atomic submarines was built at the Portsmouth Naval Shipyard, in Kittery. This was the U.S.S. *Swordfish*.

Today, Maine's forests provide paper and other wood products. Many kinds of fish come from Maine waters. Potatoes and broilers (young chickens) are major farm products.

Tourists enjoy the beautiful Maine scenery.

Tourism is also important to Maine. People from big cities like to go to Maine. They enjoy the scenery. Much of the state looks as it did when only Indians roamed the land.

Today Indians from two main tribes still live in Maine. They are the Penobscots and the Passamaquoddies (pass • ah • mah • KWAH • deez). Many of the Indians live on reservations. This is land kept especially for them. Some Indians work as nurses, teachers, or business people. But many are very poor. They survive by fishing, hunting,or working as loggers.

In 1972 Maine Indians began a legal fight. They said that their lands had been taken away unfairly, long ago. The 4,000 members of the two tribes sued the United States government. They wanted a large amount of land and money.

In 1978 Maine lawmakers and Indian leaders came to an agreement. The Indians would have some of their Maine lands returned to them. They would receive money as well.

You have learned about some of Maine's history. Now it is time for a trip—in words and pictures—through the Pine Tree State.

Imagine you are in an airplane flying high above Maine. You are flying from the north to the south. Below you, everything is green. Maine is one of our most wooded states. About 90 percent is covered by trees. That is almost the whole state. The northern part of the state is especially wooded.

You remember that many Maine trees were once cut down for shipbuilding. Lumber people thought there would always be plenty of pines. They were wrong. At one time, the Pine Tree State was nearly stripped of pine trees. New pine forests had to be planted. Now, tree cutting is a science. New trees are planted to replace the old ones that are cut down. Forest rangers watch for fires. Airplanes spray trees. The spray protects the trees from harmful insects.

Besides pines, Maine also has forests of spruce, birch, maple, beech, balsam fir, hemlock, and oak trees.

Many products we use every day began in Maine's forests. Paper is the main forest product. The paper in your books, magazines, and newspapers may have come

Potatoes
Oats
Potatoes
Forest Products
Potatoes
Dairy Products
Potatoes
Forest Products
Potatoes
Dairy Products
Forest Products
Slate
Oats
Maple Syrup
Potatoes
Sand and Gravel
Poultry
Dairy Products
Poultry
Forest Products
Forest Products
Peat
Beef Cattle
Dairy Products
Blueberries
Poultry
Feldspar
Granite
Fish
Beef Cattle
Fruit
Vegetables
Blueberries
Hogs
LEWISTON
Fish
Poultry
Limestone
Sand and Gravel
Granite
PORTLAND
Fish
Forest Products
Lobsters
Fruit

from Maine's forests. Mills in Millinocket (mill • ih • NOCK
• et), East Millinocket, Rumford (RUM • ferd), and
Woodland turn wood pulp into paper. Toothpicks,
baseball bats, and furniture are also made from Maine
lumber. Each year thousands of Maine firs become
Christmas trees.

Because of the forests, Maine has much wildlife. Black bears, beavers, foxes, mink, deer, moose, and bobcats roam through the forests and mountains. Many kinds of birds live in Maine. These include owls, ducks, chickadees, and the American bald eagle. But many of the birds fly south in the winter. Maine gets *very* cold in the winter. It once got as cold as minus 48°F.

Many deer roam through Maine's forests and mountains.

Sugarloaf Mountain

During Maine's cold, snowy winters, people ski at such places as Sugarloaf Mountain and Squaw Mountain.

As you pass over the central area of the state you'll see Maine's highest mountain—Mount Katahdin. It is almost exactly a mile high—5,268 feet tall. If you climb the mountain at dawn you will be the first person to see the sun rise over the United States. The first place the sun's rays touch the United States each morning is high atop Mount Katahdin. It is in Baxter State Park.

Blue waters of Maine's Cape Elizabeth

From an airplane, you can see the blue waters of Maine. Maine has 2,500 lakes and ponds. Maine also has more than 5,000 rivers and streams.

Along the rocky coast of Maine you see the huge Atlantic Ocean. Maine's six largest cities are strung like pearls near the ocean.

Your airplane comes down over a city in southern Maine. It is Maine's largest city—Portland. It is near the Atlantic Ocean.

Portland was first settled in about 1623. Before the town was named *Portland,* it had other names. Some were Machigonne Elbow, The Neck, Casco (KASS • coe), and Falmouth. Indians destroyed Portland twice. You remember how the town was burned during the Revolutionary War. Then in 1866 the city was hit by a large fire. Each time, Portland was rebuilt. It became a large port. It is a place where goods are sent in and out of the harbor by ship.

Today, Portland is a busy seaport. Wood and potatoes are shipped from Portland. Fishing is done in the nearby ocean. Seafood is shipped from Portland to other places. Much oil is unloaded at Portland.

There are many interesting places to visit in and around Portland. Visit Portland Head Light, in South Portland. This lighthouse was built in 1791. It helped guide ships toward shore.

Visitors can enjoy clams, lobsters, and other seafood caught in the ocean. Some enjoy walking along the rocky Atlantic shore. Others enjoy sunning themselves on the sandy beaches.

Portland is on Casco Bay. That is part of the Atlantic Ocean. There are many islands in the bay. Boat tours go to the Casco Bay Islands. According to stories, pirates buried treasures in some of the rocky Casco Bay Islands.

A famous poet, Henry Wadsworth Longfellow, was born in Portland. You can visit his boyhood home. It is the Wadsworth-Longfellow House. Tate House was built in 1775. It is Portland's oldest home.

Portland also has interesting museums. At the Maine Historical Society you can learn about Indians and early Maine settlers. The Portland Museum of Art has famous paintings. Many are seascapes.

Above left: The Portland
          Observatory
Above: The Wadsworth-
          Longfellow House
Left: Portland Head Light

Lewiston is Maine's second biggest city. Lewiston is about 35 miles north of Portland. It is on the east bank of the Androscoggin (and • roe • SKAWG • in) River, not far from the Atlantic Ocean. Textiles (fibers woven into cloth) are made in Lewiston. Think of Lewiston the next time you climb into bed. Bedspreads, pillowcases, and sheets are made in the city. Shoes are made there, too.

Nearby Auburn is called Lewiston's "Twin City." Lewiston and Auburn have many of Maine's industries. Shoes, plastics, and electric products are made in Auburn.

About 30 miles northeast of Lewiston is the capital of Maine—Augusta. Augusta lies on both sides of the Kennebec River.

This area was once a sacred land to the Indians. They held important meetings here. Augusta is very old. In 1628 Pilgrims from Massachusetts formed a fur-trading post there.

Above: The state capitol building, Augusta
Left: Blaine House, Augusta, home for Maine's
governors

In 1832 Augusta became Maine's capital. Visit the state capitol building in Augusta. There, men and women make laws for the Pine Tree State.

Fort Western is in Augusta. It was built during the French and Indian Wars. It looks much as it did over two hundred years ago. James G. Blaine ran for president of the United States in 1884. Blaine House is an interesting place to visit. It is now the home for Maine's governors.

Continue to travel northeast up the coast. You will see colorful harbors. You will see lighthouses. Off the coast you will see many lovely islands. Mount Desert Island in Acadia (ah • KAY • dee • ah) National Park is one of the most famous. Once, Abnaki Indians spent their summers around the island. They fished and caught lobsters. In 1604 Frenchman Samuel de Champlain explored the island. Today, Mount Desert Island is a vacation spot.

About 75 miles up the coast from Augusta you will come to the city of Bangor (BANG • gore). It is on the

Bailey Island

Camden Harbor

Paul Bunyan
statue, Bangor

Penobscot River. It is not far from the Atlantic Ocean.
The Jacob Buswell family were the first settlers in
Bangor in 1769. The Buswell family alone nearly made a
town. Mr. and Mrs. Buswell had nine children. Later,
Bangor became a shipbuilding city. It was also an
important lumbering center.

Today wood products, shoes, and tools are made in
Bangor.

Bangor has a giant statue of Paul Bunyan. Paul was
said to be a giant lumberjack. Lumberjacks from Maine
to Washington made up many tall stories about him.

Portland, Lewiston, Bangor, South Portland, Auburn, and Augusta are the six biggest cities in Maine. The coast of Maine has smaller interesting towns.

The oldest building in Maine is the Old Gaol Museum, in York. Today you can go in—and come out. But when it was built in 1653 the people who were put inside couldn't walk out. It was a jail.

There is an unusual house in Kennebunk (KEN • ih • bunk). According to a story, a newly married sailor had to leave his bride. He had to go out to sea. His wife had had no wedding cake. The sailor later decorated their house to look like one. It is called the Wedding Cake House.

Brunswick is the home of Bowdoin (BOH • dun) College. It was founded in 1794. Hannibal Hamlin and Henry Wadsworth Longfellow went to college there. So did Franklin Pierce, 14th president of the United States.

Bath has long been a great shipbuilding city. At the Bath Marine Museum you can learn about shipbuilding.

In Machias you can visit Burnham Tavern. During the Revolutionary War, Americans met there to plan the capture of the English ship *Margaretta*.

Above: Bath from the Kennebec River
Left: Kennebec River Lighthouse
Below left: Homes of sea captains and ship owners, Bath
Below: Bath Iron Works crew prepares a vessel for launch

Lobster boats and traps in a Maine harbor

As you travel up the coast you'll see fishing boats. They go in and out of harbors. Maine has many fleets of fishing boats. More lobsters are caught in Maine waters than in any other state. Lobster fishermen put out traps on the ocean floor. There is bait in the traps. The lobsters walk into the traps and are caught. Then the fishermen haul up the traps.

Atlantic salmon, herring, ocean perch, and scallops are also caught in the ocean waters. Clams are dug. Every day, people around the country enjoy seafood caught in Maine waters.

After going up the seacoast, visit northern Maine. Northern Maine has no big cities. But the large county that makes up northern Maine—Aroostook County—is famous for growing potatoes. Potatoes grow well where it is cool. They need plenty of water. They need soil rich in loam. Aroostook County provides all of these. It is one of the biggest potato-growing areas in the United States. The "eyes," or seeds, are planted in late spring. They are harvested in the middle of September. Sometimes, children of Aroostook County miss school because of "harvest recess." They have to help with the potato picking. In some places, machines pick the potatoes. But in many places, potatoes are still picked by hand. The potatoes leave Aroostook County by train and truck.

Maine farmers grow many other crops. Maine produces more blueberries than any of the states. Apples, oats, eggs, broiler chickens, and milk are other farm products.

Traditional church in the small Maine town of Wiscasset

Many interesting towns lie amid the forests and lakes of western Maine.

High above Earth, satellites relay television programs and telephone calls around the world. The satellite station is near the town of Andover.

At Rumford there is a big paper mill. There, wood pulp is made into paper for books.

At Paris you can see the birthplace of Hannibal Hamlin. He was vice president under Abraham Lincoln and a strong foe of slavery.

Places can't tell the whole story of Maine. This land of pine trees, lobsters, and potatoes has produced many interesting people.

You will remember that poet Henry Wadsworth Longfellow (1807-1882) was born in Portland.

The seacoast and woods of Maine have inspired many poets. Edna St. Vincent Millay (ED • nah saint VIN • cent mill • AY) and Edwin Arlington Robinson are two famous Maine poets of this century.

Writer Sarah Orne Jewett (1849-1909) was born in South Berwick, Maine. She wrote a book called *The Country of the Pointed Firs.* It is about the Maine seacoast and its people.

Artist Winslow Homer lived on the coast of Maine. He painted pictures of the sea, boats, and fishermen.

Margaret Chase Smith was born in Skowhegan (skow • HEE • gahn), Maine, in 1897. She was elected to the United States House of Representatives for four full terms. In 1948 she was elected a United States senator. She became the first woman to serve in *both* the House and Senate. She served in the Senate for 24 years—until 1973.

Seagull perches on one of Maine's coastline rocks

Edmund Sixtus Muskie was born in Rumford, Maine, in 1914. In 1954 he was elected governor of Maine. In 1958 he ran for the United States Senate. A Democrat had *never* been elected to the Senate from Maine. But Democrat Edmund Muskie won. In 1968 he ran for vice president of the United States. He was the running mate of Hubert H. Humphrey. They lost by a small margin. Back in the Senate, Edmund Muskie continues to serve Maine people.

Land of pine trees . . . potatoes . . . and lobsters.

Home to the Red Paint People . . . the Abnaki Indians . . . French . . . English . . . and American settlers.

Home to Longfellow . . . Margaret Chase Smith . . . Edmund Muskie . . . and Alice Grele.

Land where the sun first rises on the United States.

This is Maine—the Pine Tree State.

Facts About MAINE

Area—33,215 square miles (39th biggest state)

Borders—The Atlantic Ocean on the south; New Hampshire on the southwest; Canada on the northwest, north, and northeast

Greatest distance North to South—332 miles

Greatest Distance East to West—207 miles

Highest Point—5,268 feet above sea level (Mount Katahdin)

Lowest Point—Sea level (along the Atlantic Ocean coast)

Hottest Recorded Temperature—105°F. (at North Bridgton, July 10, 1911)

Coldest Recorded Temperature—Minus 48°F. (at Van Buren, on January 19, 1925)

Statehood—23rd state, on March 15, 1820

Capital—Augusta

Previous Capital—Portland

Counties—16

U.S. Senators—2

U.S. Representatives—2

Electoral Votes—4

State Senators—33

State Representatives—151

State Song—"State of Maine Song" by Roger Vinton Snow

State Motto—*Dirigo* (Latin meaning "I direct")

Nickname—Pine Tree State

Origin of Name Maine—Used by early fishermen to distinguish the *Main* land from the islands off the shore

State Seal—Adopted in 1820

State Flag—Adopted in 1909

State Flower—White pine cone and tassel

State Tree—White pine

State Animal—Moose

State Bird—Chickadee

State Fish—Landlocked salmon

State Insect—Honey bee

State Mineral—Tourmaline

Principal Rivers—Androscoggin, Kennebec, Penobscot, Saco, St. John, St. Croix

Largest Lake—Moosehead Lake

Farm Products—Potatoes, eggs, broiler chickens, milk, beef cattle, hogs, sheep, oats, apples, blueberries, strawberries

Fishing—Lobsters, clams, ocean perch, scallops, sea herring, shrimps

Manufacturing—Paper products, wood products, food products, leather products, ships, machinery, textiles

Mining—Sand, gravel, granite, zinc
Population—1980 census: 1,124,660 (1993 estimate: 1,204,500)
Population Density—34 people per square mile
Population Distribution—51 percent urban; 49 percent rural

Major Cities	1980 Census	1990 Estimate
Portland	61,572	61,059
Lewiston	40,481	39,728
Bangor	31,643	32,368
Auburn	23,128	22,566
South Portland	22,712	not available
Augusta	21,819	21,567

MAINE HISTORY

People came to Maine at least 10,000 years ago; about 4,000 years ago
ancient people known as the Red Paint People lived in Maine; when
Europeans arrived, Abnaki and Etchemin Indians lived there
About 1000 A.D.—It is thought that Vikings, led by Leif Ericson, explored the
coast of Maine about this time
1498—It is thought that John Cabot sailed close to the Maine coast for
England
1524—Giovanni da Verrazano explores Maine for France

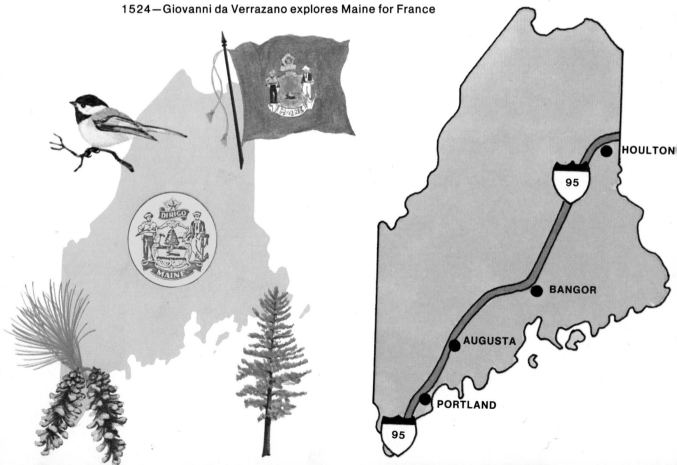

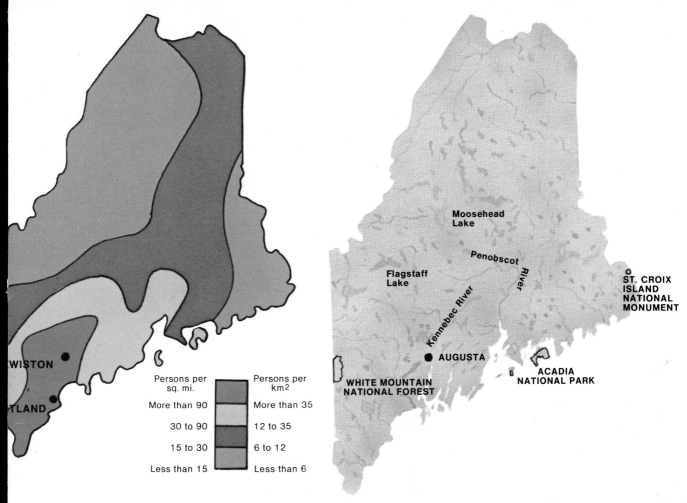

Persons per sq. mi. | Persons per km2
More than 90 | More than 35
30 to 90 | 12 to 35
15 to 30 | 6 to 12
Less than 15 | Less than 6

1569 — English sailors walk on Maine soil

1604 — Samuel de Champlain explores Mount Desert for France

1605 — Englishman George Weymouth kidnaps five Indians and takes them to England

1607 — Popham Colony is first English attempt to colonize New England; the settlement is unsuccessful

1622 — Maine lands are granted by King of England to Sir Ferdinando Gorges and John Mason

1629 — Gorges and Mason divide their lands; Gorges receives Maine and Mason receives New Hampshire

1641 — English city Gorgeana (the present city of York) becomes the first chartered English city in America

1677 — The colony of Massachusetts buys Maine from the Gorges family for about $6,000

1688 — Beginning of French and Indian Wars

1691 — Maine becomes the District of Maine under the control of the Massachusetts colony

1763 — English win French and Indian Wars and control Maine

1764 — About 24,000 settlers live in Maine

45

1774—Maine people in Saco, Falmouth, and Machias protest English taxes

1775—Revolutionary War begins on April 19; Falmouth (now Portland) is burned by English ships; English ship *Margaretta* is captured by Americans at Machias

1783—Americans win Revolutionary War; new country has been born—the United States of America

1788—Slavery is abolished in Maine and Massachusetts

1791—Portland Head Light, the oldest lighthouse on the Atlantic coast, is established

1794—Bowdoin College is established

1800—Population of Maine is 151,719

1807—Henry Wadsworth Longfellow is born at Portland on February 27

1809—Hannibal Hamlin, United States vice president from 1861-1865, is born at Paris on August 27

1820—Maine becomes our 23rd state on March 15!

1832—Augusta is new capital

1839—"Aroostook War"—battle over Maine-Canada border—begins

1842—Webster-Ashburton Treaty settles Maine-Canada border dispute

1850—Population of Pine Tree State is 583,169

1861-1865—Civil War, Maine sends 72,945 men to fight for North

1866—Great Portland fire on July 4 almost destroys city

1900—Population of Pine Tree State is 694,466

1917—United States enters World War I; over 35,000 Maine men and women serve

1919—Acadia National Park, the only national park in New England, is created by Congress (first called Lafayette National Park)

1920—Happy 100th birthday, Pine Tree State!

1936—Floods hit Maine

1941-1945—During World War II, over 95,000 Maine men and women serve in armed forces; many ships are built in Maine shipyards

1958—Edmund S. Muskie, born in Rumford, becomes first Democrat ever elected to the United States Senate from Maine

1962—Satellite Station built near Andover

1968—Edmund Muskie is the Democratic vice-presidential candidate, but he and Hubert Humphrey lose to Nixon and Agnew

1972—Penobscot and Passamaquoddy Indians file suit claiming their lands were unjustly taken from them

1978—Maine lawmakers and Indian leaders reach agreement

1980—Edmund S. Muskie becomes our country's Secretary of State, U.S. government agrees to pay the Penobscot and Passamaquoddy Indians $81½ million in payment for land seizures of 1700s and 1800s.

1987—John R. McKernan, Jr. begins first term as governor

INDEX

47

About the Author:

Dennis Fradin attended Northwestern University on a creative writing scholarship and was graduated in 1967. While still at Northwestern, he published his first stories in *Ingenue* magazine and also won a prize in *Seventeen's* short story competition. A prolific writer, Dennis Fradin has been regularly publishing stories in such diverse places as *The Saturday Evening Post, Scholastic, National Humane Review, Midwest,* and *The Teaching Paper.* He has also scripted several educational films. Since 1970 he has taught second grade reading in a Chicago school—a rewarding job, which, the author says, "provides a captive audience on whom I test my children's stories." Married and the father of three children, Dennis Fradin spends his free time with his family or playing a myriad of sports and games with his childhood chums.

About the Artists:

Len Meents studied painting and drawing at Southern Illinois University and after graduation in 1969 he moved to Chicago. Mr. Meents works full time as a painter and illustrator. He and his wife and child currently make their home in LaGrange, Illinois.

Richard Wahl, graduate of the Art Center College of Design in Los Angeles, has illustrated a number of magazine articles and booklets. He is a skilled artist and photographer who advocates realistic interpretations of his subjects. He lives with his wife and two sons in Libertyville, Illinois.